Truck Mania

By Ed and Ruth Radlauer

AN ELK GROVE BOOK

CHILDRENS PRESS, CHICAGO

STRATEGIES, a teaching guide for using *MANIA BOOKS* for reading instruction, is available along with a cassette recording and *MANIA CARDS* (skill-builders) to accompany this book.

Photo credits:
   Freightliner Corporation, Portland, Oregon, pp. 20, 21

Library of Congress Cataloging in Publication Data

Radlauer, Ed.
   Truck mania.
   (Mania books)
   ''An Elk Grove book.''
   Includes index.
   Summary: Uses simple vocabulary to discuss trucks and their parts.
   1. Trucks—Juvenile literature. [1. Trucks]
I. Radlauer, Ruth Shaw. II. Title.
III. Series: Radlauer mania book.
TL230.R34   629.2'24   81-15448
ISBN 0-516-07790-2   AACR2

A RADLAUER
Mania Book

CREATED FOR CHILDRENS PRESS BY
*RADLAUER PRODUCTIONS INCORPORATED

Truck mania?
Yes, it's truck mania.

There you go
on four truck wheels.

You can go
on four wheels—

—or on six big wheels.

Six big wheels can
do a lot of work.

You need lots of wheels
to do lots of work.
Lots of wheels?

Your semi needs
a tractor—

—and trailers.

Your big rig tractor—

—can pull a trailer.

A truck needs
an engine.

Your big rig needs gears.
The engine and gears
do lots of work.

To do lots of work,
the truck engine needs
lots of horsepower.

Yes, a truck needs horsepower.

Your truck—

—needs lots of
pieces and parts.

The cab has lots of
pieces and parts.

The cab and tractor
have lots of
pieces and parts.

Some trucks—

—can dump.

Trucks carry
and dump.

Can a truck
carry a dump truck?

Your truck needs a name.

A truck needs a name?

Big rigs have
gears, cabs, and
eighteen wheels.

Eighteen wheels?

Yes, it's
truck mania.

And there you
go on two wheels.
On two wheels?

Truck words